50 Sweet and Savories Recipes for Home

By: Kelly Johnson

Table of Contents

- Chocolate-covered strawberries
- Caprese salad skewers
- Lemon-blueberry scones
- Spinach and feta stuffed mushrooms
- Raspberry almond tart
- Prosciutto-wrapped asparagus
- Vanilla bean panna cotta
- Mini quiches with smoked salmon
- Cinnamon sugar pretzel bites
- Tomato basil bruschetta
- Maple-bacon-wrapped dates
- Strawberry shortcake cupcakes
- Brie and cranberry puff pastry bites
- Blueberry balsamic glaze chicken wings
- Dark chocolate-dipped pretzels
- Shrimp and mango summer rolls
- Raspberry-chocolate mousse cups
- Parmesan garlic roasted chickpeas
- Peach and prosciutto flatbread
- Mini cheesecake bites
- Sweet potato fries with garlic aioli
- Pomegranate and goat cheese crostini
- Honey mustard glazed chicken skewers
- Lemon poppy seed muffins
- Caprese-stuffed avocados
- Salted caramel brownie bites
- Roasted red pepper hummus
- Apple pecan brie bites
- Mini key lime pies
- Bacon-wrapped jalapeño poppers
- Nutella-filled crescent rolls
- Teriyaki chicken lettuce wraps
- Pistachio and cranberry biscotti
- Artichoke and parmesan dip
- Chocolate chip cookie dough truffles

- Greek salad cups
- Raspberry cheesecake bars
- Spicy honey glazed shrimp
- Caramel apple hand pies
- Mini chicken pot pies
- Cheddar and chive potato skins
- Blueberry goat cheese crostini
- Cinnamon sugar apple chips
- BBQ pulled pork sliders
- Nutella banana spring rolls
- Bacon-wrapped figs with goat cheese
- Lemon rosemary roasted nuts
- Pesto and sun-dried tomato pinwheels
- Cranberry orange shortbread cookies
- Teriyaki pineapple chicken skewers

Chocolate-covered strawberries

Ingredients:

- 1 pound fresh strawberries, washed and dried
- 8 ounces dark chocolate, chopped
- 2 tablespoons unsalted butter
- 1 teaspoon vanilla extract
- Optional toppings: chopped nuts, shredded coconut, sprinkles

Instructions:

Line a baking sheet with parchment paper.
In a heatproof bowl, melt the dark chocolate and butter together. You can do this over a double boiler or in the microwave, stirring in 20-second intervals until smooth.
Stir in the vanilla extract into the melted chocolate mixture.
Hold each strawberry by the stem and dip it into the melted chocolate, ensuring it's well-coated. Allow excess chocolate to drip off.
Place the dipped strawberries on the prepared baking sheet.
If desired, sprinkle the dipped strawberries with chopped nuts, shredded coconut, or sprinkles while the chocolate is still wet.
Allow the chocolate-covered strawberries to set at room temperature or in the refrigerator for about 30 minutes, or until the chocolate hardens.
Once set, transfer the strawberries to a serving plate and enjoy!

Note: You can get creative with the toppings and even drizzle additional melted white or milk chocolate over the dipped strawberries for an extra touch.

Caprese salad skewers

Ingredients:

- Cherry tomatoes
- Fresh mozzarella balls (bocconcini)
- Fresh basil leaves
- Balsamic glaze
- Olive oil
- Salt and pepper, to taste
- Skewers or toothpicks

Instructions:

Rinse the cherry tomatoes and basil leaves. Drain the mozzarella balls if they are stored in liquid.

Assemble the skewers by sliding a cherry tomato onto the skewer, followed by a folded basil leaf and a mozzarella ball. Repeat the pattern until the skewer is filled.

Arrange the assembled caprese skewers on a serving platter.

Drizzle balsamic glaze and olive oil over the skewers. You can adjust the amount according to your taste.

Sprinkle salt and pepper over the skewers for seasoning.

Serve the caprese salad skewers immediately, or refrigerate them until ready to serve. Enjoy this delightful and refreshing appetizer!

Lemon-blueberry scones

Ingredients:

- 2 cups all-purpose flour
- 1/2 cup granulated sugar
- 1 tablespoon baking powder
- 1/2 teaspoon salt
- 1/2 cup unsalted butter, cold and cut into small pieces
- 1 cup fresh or frozen blueberries
- Zest of 1 lemon
- 1/2 cup milk
- 1 large egg
- 1 teaspoon vanilla extract
- Optional: Lemon Glaze (1 cup powdered sugar, 2 tablespoons lemon juice)

Instructions:

Preheat your oven to 400°F (200°C). Line a baking sheet with parchment paper.
In a large bowl, whisk together the flour, sugar, baking powder, and salt.
Add the cold, diced butter to the dry ingredients. Use a pastry cutter or your fingertips to cut the butter into the flour mixture until it resembles coarse crumbs.
Gently fold in the blueberries and lemon zest.
In a separate bowl, whisk together the milk, egg, and vanilla extract.
Make a well in the center of the dry ingredients and pour the wet ingredients into it. Stir until just combined. Be careful not to overmix; the dough should be slightly crumbly.
Turn the dough out onto a floured surface and gently knead it a few times to bring it together. Pat the dough into a circle about 1 inch (2.5 cm) thick.
Use a sharp knife to cut the circle into 8 wedges. Place the scones on the prepared baking sheet, leaving some space between each.
Bake for 15-18 minutes or until the scones are golden brown and cooked through.
Optional: While the scones are cooling, mix together the powdered sugar and lemon juice to create a glaze. Drizzle the glaze over the cooled scones.
Allow the scones to cool slightly before serving. Enjoy these lemon-blueberry scones with a hot cup of tea or coffee!

Spinach and feta stuffed mushrooms

Ingredients:

- 20 large button mushrooms, stems removed and reserved
- 2 tablespoons olive oil
- 1 small onion, finely chopped
- 2 cloves garlic, minced
- 2 cups fresh spinach, chopped
- 1/2 cup crumbled feta cheese
- Salt and pepper, to taste
- 1/4 cup breadcrumbs (optional, for topping)
- Fresh parsley, chopped (for garnish)

Instructions:

Preheat the oven to 375°F (190°C). Line a baking sheet with parchment paper. Clean the mushrooms and remove the stems. Finely chop the mushroom stems and set aside.

In a large skillet, heat olive oil over medium heat. Add the chopped onion and cook until softened, about 3-4 minutes.

Add the minced garlic to the skillet and cook for an additional 1-2 minutes until fragrant.

Add the chopped mushroom stems to the skillet and cook for 3-4 minutes until they release their moisture.

Stir in the chopped spinach and cook until wilted. Season with salt and pepper to taste.

Remove the skillet from the heat and let the mixture cool for a few minutes. Once cooled, stir in the crumbled feta cheese.

Stuff each mushroom cap with the spinach and feta mixture, placing them on the prepared baking sheet.

Optional: Sprinkle breadcrumbs over the stuffed mushrooms for added texture.

Bake in the preheated oven for 15-20 minutes or until the mushrooms are tender and the filling is golden brown.

Garnish with fresh parsley and serve warm. These spinach and feta stuffed mushrooms make a delicious appetizer or side dish. Enjoy!

Raspberry almond tart

Ingredients:

For the Almond Crust:

- 1 cup all-purpose flour
- 1/2 cup ground almonds
- 1/4 cup granulated sugar
- 1/2 cup unsalted butter, cold and cut into small pieces
- 1 large egg yolk
- 1 tablespoon ice water

For the Almond Cream Filling:

- 1/2 cup unsalted butter, softened
- 1/2 cup granulated sugar
- 1 cup ground almonds
- 2 large eggs
- 1 teaspoon almond extract

For Topping:

- 1 cup fresh raspberries
- Powdered sugar for dusting

Instructions:

1. Almond Crust:

    In a food processor, combine the flour, ground almonds, and sugar. Pulse to mix. Add the cold butter pieces and pulse until the mixture resembles coarse crumbs. In a small bowl, whisk together the egg yolk and ice water. Add this mixture to the food processor and pulse until the dough comes together.
    Turn the dough out onto a lightly floured surface, knead it briefly to bring it together, then shape it into a disk. Wrap in plastic wrap and refrigerate for at least 30 minutes.

2. Almond Cream Filling:

    In a bowl, cream together the softened butter and sugar until light and fluffy.

Add the ground almonds, eggs, and almond extract. Mix until well combined. Set aside.

3. Assembly:

Preheat the oven to 350°F (180°C).
Roll out the chilled almond crust on a floured surface to fit a tart pan. Press the dough into the tart pan, ensuring an even layer.
Spread the almond cream filling over the crust.
Bake in the preheated oven for 25-30 minutes or until the almond filling is set and the crust is golden brown.
Allow the tart to cool completely.

4. Topping:

Once cooled, arrange fresh raspberries on top of the almond cream.
Dust the tart with powdered sugar for a finishing touch.

5. Serving:

Slice and serve the raspberry almond tart at room temperature.
Enjoy this delightful combination of almond cream and fresh raspberries!

Prosciutto-wrapped asparagus

Ingredients:

- 1 bunch fresh asparagus spears, trimmed
- 1 tablespoon olive oil
- Salt and black pepper, to taste
- 10-12 slices prosciutto

Instructions:

Preheat your oven to 400°F (200°C). Line a baking sheet with parchment paper.
Toss the trimmed asparagus spears with olive oil, salt, and black pepper in a bowl until well-coated.
Take a slice of prosciutto and wrap it around each asparagus spear, starting from the bottom and spiraling upward. Repeat with the remaining asparagus.
Place the prosciutto-wrapped asparagus spears on the prepared baking sheet.

Bake in the preheated oven for 12-15 minutes or until the asparagus is tender and the prosciutto is crispy.

Optional: For a finishing touch, you can drizzle a little extra olive oil over the asparagus before serving.

Serve the prosciutto-wrapped asparagus as a delicious appetizer or side dish. Enjoy the combination of salty prosciutto and fresh asparagus!

Vanilla bean panna cotta

Ingredients:

For the Panna Cotta:

- 2 cups heavy cream
- 1/2 cup granulated sugar
- 1 vanilla bean pod, split lengthwise (or 2 teaspoons pure vanilla extract)
- 2 1/4 teaspoons unflavored gelatin
- 3 tablespoons cold water

For the Vanilla Bean Sauce:

- 1/4 cup water
- 1/4 cup granulated sugar
- 1 vanilla bean pod, split lengthwise (or 1 teaspoon pure vanilla extract)

Instructions:

1. Panna Cotta:

    In a saucepan, combine the heavy cream and sugar over medium heat. Scrape the seeds from the vanilla bean pod and add both the seeds and the pod to the mixture. Alternatively, if using vanilla extract, add it later.
    Stir the mixture until it is just about to simmer (do not let it boil). Remove it from the heat.

3. Gelatin Mixture:

    In a small bowl, sprinkle the gelatin over the cold water. Let it sit for 5 minutes to bloom.

4. Combine and Strain:

    Remove the vanilla bean pod from the cream mixture.
    Microwave the gelatin mixture for about 15 seconds or until it turns into a clear liquid.
    Stir the gelatin mixture into the warm cream until fully dissolved. If using vanilla extract, add it at this point and mix well.

Strain the mixture through a fine-mesh sieve into a pouring jug to remove any vanilla bean particles.

5. Pour into Molds:

    Divide the mixture evenly among serving glasses or ramekins.
    Refrigerate for at least 4 hours or until set.

6. Vanilla Bean Sauce:

    In a small saucepan, combine water and sugar over medium heat. Scrape the seeds from the vanilla bean pod and add both the seeds and the pod to the mixture. Alternatively, if using vanilla extract, add it later.
    Stir until the sugar is dissolved, and the mixture has slightly thickened.
    Remove from heat and let it cool. Strain the sauce to remove the vanilla bean particles.

7. Serving:

    Once the panna cotta is set, spoon the vanilla bean sauce over the top.
    Optionally, garnish with fresh berries or mint leaves.
    Serve and enjoy this creamy and indulgent vanilla bean panna cotta!

Mini quiches with smoked salmon

Ingredients:

For the Quiche Filling:

- 1 cup smoked salmon, diced
- 1/2 cup cream cheese, softened
- 1/4 cup sour cream
- 3 large eggs
- 1/4 cup chives, finely chopped
- Salt and black pepper, to taste

For the Pie Crust:

- 1 1/4 cups all-purpose flour
- 1/2 cup unsalted butter, cold and diced
- 1/4 teaspoon salt
- 3-4 tablespoons ice water

Optional Garnish:

- Fresh dill
- Extra chives

Instructions:

1. Pie Crust:

    In a food processor, combine the flour, cold diced butter, and salt. Pulse until the mixture resembles coarse crumbs.
    Add ice water, one tablespoon at a time, and pulse until the dough just comes together.
    Turn the dough out onto a floured surface, shape it into a disk, wrap in plastic wrap, and refrigerate for at least 30 minutes.

2. Quiche Filling:

    Preheat the oven to 375°F (190°C).
    In a bowl, mix together the diced smoked salmon, softened cream cheese, sour cream, eggs, chives, salt, and black pepper until well combined.

3. Assembly:

   Roll out the chilled pie crust on a floured surface and cut out small rounds to fit your mini muffin tin.
   Press the rounds into the mini muffin tin to form crusts.
   Spoon the smoked salmon and cream cheese filling into each crust.

4. Baking:

   Bake in the preheated oven for about 15-20 minutes or until the quiches are set and the crust is golden brown.
   Allow the mini quiches to cool slightly before removing them from the muffin tin.

5. Garnish:

   Garnish each mini quiche with fresh dill and extra chopped chives.

6. Serving:

   Serve these delightful mini quiches with smoked salmon as a delicious appetizer or brunch dish.

Enjoy these bite-sized treats with the rich flavors of smoked salmon and cream cheese!

Cinnamon sugar pretzel bites

Ingredients:

For the Pretzel Dough:

- 1 1/2 cups warm water (110°F/43°C)
- 1 tablespoon granulated sugar
- 2 teaspoons active dry yeast
- 4 cups all-purpose flour
- 1 teaspoon salt
- 2 tablespoons unsalted butter, melted

For the Cinnamon Sugar Coating:

- 1/2 cup unsalted butter, melted
- 1 cup granulated sugar
- 2 tablespoons ground cinnamon

For the Optional Dip:

- Cream cheese frosting or chocolate sauce

Instructions:

1. Pretzel Dough:

    In a bowl, combine warm water and sugar. Sprinkle the yeast over the water and let it sit for about 5 minutes, or until foamy.
    In a large mixing bowl, combine the flour and salt. Pour in the yeast mixture and melted butter. Mix until the dough comes together.
    Knead the dough on a floured surface for about 5 minutes until it becomes smooth and elastic. Place the dough in a greased bowl, cover it with a clean cloth, and let it rise in a warm place for about 1 hour or until doubled in size.

2. Forming Pretzel Bites:

    Preheat the oven to 425°F (220°C). Line a baking sheet with parchment paper.
    Punch down the risen dough and turn it out onto a floured surface.
    Divide the dough into small sections and roll each section into a long rope.
    Cut the ropes into bite-sized pieces (about 1 inch each).

3. Pretzel Bath:

    In a large pot, bring water to a boil. Reduce the heat to a simmer.
    Carefully add the pretzel bites to the simmering water for about 20-30 seconds.
    Remove them with a slotted spoon and place them on the prepared baking sheet.

4. Baking:

    Bake the pretzel bites in the preheated oven for 10-12 minutes or until golden brown.
    While the pretzel bites are baking, prepare the cinnamon sugar coating.

5. Cinnamon Sugar Coating:

    In a bowl, mix together the granulated sugar and ground cinnamon.
    Dip each pretzel bite into the melted butter and then roll it in the cinnamon sugar mixture until well coated.

6. Serving:

    Allow the pretzel bites to cool slightly before serving.
    Optionally, serve with cream cheese frosting or chocolate sauce for dipping.

Enjoy these delicious homemade cinnamon sugar pretzel bites as a sweet and satisfying treat!

Tomato basil bruschetta

Ingredients:

- 4-5 ripe tomatoes, diced
- 1/4 cup fresh basil leaves, finely chopped
- 2 cloves garlic, minced
- 2 tablespoons extra virgin olive oil
- 1 tablespoon balsamic vinegar
- Salt and black pepper, to taste
- Baguette or Italian bread, sliced

Instructions:

In a bowl, combine the diced tomatoes, chopped basil, minced garlic, olive oil, and balsamic vinegar.

Season the mixture with salt and black pepper to taste. Mix well to ensure all the ingredients are evenly coated.

Allow the tomato basil mixture to marinate for at least 15-20 minutes to let the flavors meld together.

Preheat your oven broiler or a grill pan.

Arrange the sliced baguette or Italian bread on a baking sheet. If using a grill pan, you can brush the bread with a little olive oil.

Toast the bread under the broiler or on the grill pan until golden brown on each side. Keep an eye on them to prevent burning.

Once the bread is toasted, spoon the tomato basil mixture onto each slice.

Serve immediately as a delightful appetizer or snack.

Enjoy the fresh and vibrant flavors of tomato basil bruschetta on crispy bread!

Maple-bacon-wrapped dates

Ingredients:

- 16 large Medjool dates, pitted
- 8 slices bacon, cut in half
- 1/4 cup maple syrup
- Toothpicks or small skewers

Instructions:

Preheat your oven to 375°F (190°C). Line a baking sheet with parchment paper.
Carefully make a small slit in each date to remove the pit, creating a cavity for stuffing.
Place a small amount of maple syrup inside each date, ensuring they are well-coated.
Take a half-slice of bacon and wrap it around each date, securing it with a toothpick or small skewer.
Arrange the bacon-wrapped dates on the prepared baking sheet, with the seam side down.
Drizzle any remaining maple syrup over the bacon-wrapped dates.
Bake in the preheated oven for 15-20 minutes or until the bacon is crispy, turning halfway through to ensure even cooking.
Once cooked, remove the toothpicks or skewers and let the maple-bacon-wrapped dates cool for a few minutes before serving.
Serve these sweet and savory treats as an appetizer or party snack.

Enjoy the irresistible combination of sweet dates, smoky bacon, and maple syrup!

Strawberry shortcake cupcakes

Ingredients:

For the Cupcakes:

- 1 1/2 cups all-purpose flour
- 1 1/2 teaspoons baking powder
- 1/4 teaspoon salt
- 1/2 cup unsalted butter, softened
- 1 cup granulated sugar
- 2 large eggs
- 1 teaspoon vanilla extract
- 1/2 cup whole milk

For the Strawberry Filling:

- 1 1/2 cups fresh strawberries, hulled and diced
- 2 tablespoons granulated sugar

For the Whipped Cream Frosting:

- 1 cup heavy cream, chilled
- 1/4 cup powdered sugar
- 1 teaspoon vanilla extract

For Assembly:

- Additional fresh strawberries for garnish

Instructions:

1. Cupcakes:

> Preheat the oven to 350°F (175°C). Line a muffin tin with cupcake liners.
> In a medium bowl, whisk together the flour, baking powder, and salt. Set aside.
> In a large bowl, cream together the softened butter and sugar until light and fluffy.
> Add the eggs one at a time, beating well after each addition. Stir in the vanilla extract.

Gradually add the dry ingredients to the wet ingredients, alternating with the milk, beginning and ending with the dry ingredients. Mix until just combined.
Divide the batter evenly among the cupcake liners, filling each about two-thirds full.
Bake in the preheated oven for 18-20 minutes or until a toothpick inserted into the center comes out clean.
Allow the cupcakes to cool completely before filling and frosting.

2. Strawberry Filling:

In a bowl, combine the diced strawberries and granulated sugar. Let them sit for at least 15-20 minutes to release their juices.

3. Whipped Cream Frosting:

In a chilled bowl, whip the heavy cream until it starts to thicken.
Add the powdered sugar and vanilla extract. Continue whipping until stiff peaks form.

4. Assembly:

Once the cupcakes are completely cooled, use a knife or cupcake corer to create a small hole in the center of each cupcake.
Fill each hole with the macerated strawberry mixture.
Pipe or spread the whipped cream frosting on top of each cupcake.
Garnish with additional fresh strawberries.
Chill the cupcakes in the refrigerator for at least 30 minutes before serving.

Enjoy these delightful strawberry shortcake cupcakes with a perfect balance of sweetness and freshness!

Brie and cranberry puff pastry bites

Ingredients:

- 1 sheet puff pastry, thawed
- 1/2 cup cranberry sauce (homemade or store-bought)
- 150g Brie cheese, cut into small cubes
- 1 egg, beaten (for egg wash)
- Fresh rosemary or thyme for garnish (optional)

Instructions:

Preheat your oven to 400°F (200°C). Line a baking sheet with parchment paper
On a lightly floured surface, roll out the puff pastry sheet to smooth out any creases.
Using a sharp knife or a pastry cutter, cut the puff pastry into small squares, about 2 inches by 2 inches.
Place the puff pastry squares on the prepared baking sheet, leaving some space between each.
Spoon a small amount of cranberry sauce onto the center of each puff pastry square.
Top the cranberry sauce with a cube of Brie cheese.
Fold the corners of each puff pastry square towards the center, creating a small, sealed puff pastry bite.
Brush the exposed puff pastry with beaten egg for a golden finish.
Bake in the preheated oven for 12-15 minutes or until the puff pastry is golden and puffed.
Remove from the oven and let the bites cool for a few minutes.
Optionally, garnish with fresh rosemary or thyme.
Serve these Brie and cranberry puff pastry bites warm as a delicious appetizer for your guests.

Enjoy the combination of the creamy Brie, sweet cranberry, and flaky puff pastry in every bite!

Blueberry balsamic glaze chicken wings

Ingredients:

For the Chicken Wings:

- 2 pounds chicken wings, split at joints, tips discarded
- Salt and black pepper, to taste
- 1 tablespoon olive oil
- 1 teaspoon garlic powder
- 1 teaspoon onion powder
- 1 teaspoon smoked paprika

For the Blueberry Balsamic Glaze:

- 1 cup fresh or frozen blueberries
- 1/4 cup balsamic vinegar
- 2 tablespoons honey
- 1 tablespoon soy sauce
- 1 teaspoon Dijon mustard
- 1 clove garlic, minced
- Salt and black pepper, to taste

Optional Garnish:

- Fresh blueberries
- Chopped fresh cilantro or parsley

Instructions:

1. Chicken Wings:

    Preheat your oven to 400°F (200°C). Line a baking sheet with parchment paper.
    In a large bowl, toss the chicken wings with olive oil, salt, black pepper, garlic powder, onion powder, and smoked paprika until evenly coated.
    Arrange the seasoned chicken wings on the prepared baking sheet in a single layer.
    Bake in the preheated oven for 45-50 minutes or until the wings are crispy and golden brown, turning them halfway through the cooking time.

2. Blueberry Balsamic Glaze:

In a saucepan over medium heat, combine the blueberries, balsamic vinegar, honey, soy sauce, Dijon mustard, minced garlic, salt, and black pepper.

Bring the mixture to a simmer, then reduce the heat to low. Allow it to simmer for about 10-15 minutes, stirring occasionally, until the blueberries break down, and the sauce thickens.

Use a spoon or immersion blender to puree the blueberry mixture until smooth.

Strain the mixture through a fine-mesh sieve to remove any remaining solids.

3. Glazing the Wings:

Once the chicken wings are cooked, transfer them to a large bowl.

Pour the blueberry balsamic glaze over the chicken wings and toss until they are evenly coated.

Garnish with fresh blueberries and chopped cilantro or parsley, if desired.

Serve the blueberry balsamic glaze chicken wings immediately, and enjoy the unique and flavorful combination of sweet and tangy glaze!

Dark chocolate-dipped pretzels

Ingredients:

- 1 cup dark chocolate chips or chopped dark chocolate
- 2 tablespoons coconut oil or vegetable shortening
- Pretzel rods or pretzel twists

Instructions:

Line a baking sheet with parchment paper.

In a heatproof bowl, combine the dark chocolate and coconut oil or vegetable shortening.

Melt the chocolate in the microwave or using a double boiler. If using the microwave, heat in 20-second intervals, stirring between each interval until the chocolate is fully melted and smooth.

Once the chocolate is melted, let it cool slightly for a few minutes to avoid overheating the pretzels.

Dip each pretzel rod or pretzel twist into the melted chocolate, coating it evenly. Use a spoon to help coat the pretzel if needed.

Allow any excess chocolate to drip off, and place the chocolate-covered pretzel on the prepared baking sheet.

Repeat the dipping process with the remaining pretzels.

Place the baking sheet in the refrigerator for about 15-20 minutes or until the chocolate coating is set.

Once the chocolate is set, remove the pretzels from the refrigerator.

If desired, you can drizzle additional melted chocolate over the chocolate-dipped pretzels or sprinkle them with toppings like crushed nuts, sprinkles, or sea salt while the chocolate is still wet.

Let the pretzels come to room temperature before serving.

Enjoy these delicious dark chocolate-dipped pretzels as a sweet and salty treat!

Shrimp and mango summer rolls

Ingredients:

For the Summer Rolls:

- Rice paper wrappers
- 16 large shrimp, cooked, peeled, and deveined
- 1 mango, peeled, pitted, and thinly sliced
- 1 cucumber, julienned
- 1 carrot, julienned
- Fresh mint leaves
- Fresh cilantro leaves
- Rice vermicelli, cooked according to package instructions

For the Dipping Sauce:

- 1/4 cup hoisin sauce
- 2 tablespoons peanut butter
- 1 tablespoon soy sauce
- 1 tablespoon lime juice
- 1 teaspoon Sriracha (optional)
- 2-3 tablespoons water (to thin the sauce)

Instructions:

1. Prepare Ingredients:

    Cook the shrimp, peel, and devein them. Cut each shrimp in half lengthwise. Prepare all the vegetables and herbs by washing, peeling, and julienning as needed.
    Cook the rice vermicelli according to the package instructions, and let it cool.

2. Dipping Sauce:

    In a small bowl, whisk together hoisin sauce, peanut butter, soy sauce, lime juice, and Sriracha (if using).

Add water gradually until you reach your desired consistency. Mix until well combined.

Adjust the taste by adding more lime juice, soy sauce, or Sriracha as needed. Set aside.

3. Assemble Summer Rolls:

Fill a shallow dish with warm water. Dip one rice paper wrapper into the water, rotating it for about 10-15 seconds until it becomes pliable.

Lay the softened rice paper on a clean, damp surface.

Place a few shrimp halves, slices of mango, julienned cucumber, carrot, a small amount of rice vermicelli, mint leaves, and cilantro leaves in the center of the wrapper.

Fold the sides of the rice paper over the filling, then fold the bottom and roll tightly, similar to a burrito.

Repeat the process with the remaining ingredients.

4. Serve:

Arrange the shrimp and mango summer rolls on a serving plate.

Serve the rolls with the prepared dipping sauce on the side.

Optionally, garnish with extra fresh herbs or a sprinkle of sesame seeds.

Enjoy these refreshing and flavorful shrimp and mango summer rolls as a light and delicious appetizer or meal!

Raspberry-chocolate mousse cups

Ingredients:

For the Chocolate Mousse:

- 1 cup dark chocolate, finely chopped
- 2 cups heavy cream
- 1/4 cup granulated sugar
- 1 teaspoon vanilla extract

For the Raspberry Sauce:

- 1 cup fresh raspberries
- 2 tablespoons sugar
- 1 tablespoon water
- 1 teaspoon lemon juice

For Assembly:

- Fresh raspberries for garnish
- Chocolate shavings or cocoa powder for garnish (optional)

Instructions:

1. Chocolate Mousse:

    Melt the dark chocolate in a heatproof bowl over simmering water or in the microwave. Allow it to cool slightly.
    In a separate bowl, whip the heavy cream until soft peaks form. Add sugar and vanilla extract and continue whipping until stiff peaks form.
    Gently fold the melted chocolate into the whipped cream until well combined. Be careful not to deflate the whipped cream.
    Refrigerate the chocolate mousse for at least 2 hours to allow it to set.

2. Raspberry Sauce:

    In a small saucepan, combine fresh raspberries, sugar, water, and lemon juice.
    Cook over medium heat, stirring occasionally, until the raspberries break down and the sauce thickens. This usually takes about 8-10 minutes.
    Once the sauce has thickened, remove it from heat and strain it through a fine mesh sieve to remove seeds. Allow it to cool.

3. Assembly:
- Take small serving cups or glasses for assembling the mousse cups.
- Spoon a layer of chocolate mousse into the bottom of each cup.
- Add a layer of raspberry sauce on top of the chocolate mousse.
- Repeat the layers until the cups are filled, finishing with a dollop of chocolate mousse on top.
- Garnish with fresh raspberries and chocolate shavings or cocoa powder if desired.
- Refrigerate the raspberry-chocolate mousse cups for at least an hour before serving to allow the flavors to meld and the dessert to set.

Enjoy these decadent raspberry-chocolate mousse cups as a delightful ending to a special meal or as a treat for any occasion!

Parmesan garlic roasted chickpeas

Ingredients:

- 2 cans (15 ounces each) chickpeas (garbanzo beans), drained and rinsed
- 2 tablespoons olive oil
- 1/2 cup grated Parmesan cheese
- 2 teaspoons garlic powder
- 1 teaspoon onion powder
- 1 teaspoon dried oregano
- 1/2 teaspoon salt (adjust to taste)
- 1/4 teaspoon black pepper
- Optional: Red pepper flakes for a bit of heat

Instructions:

Preheat the Oven:
- Preheat your oven to 400°F (200°C).

Prepare the Chickpeas:
- Rinse and drain the canned chickpeas. Pat them dry with a paper towel to remove excess moisture. You can also peel the chickpeas for a crunchier texture.

Seasoning Mixture:
- In a bowl, mix together olive oil, grated Parmesan cheese, garlic powder, onion powder, dried oregano, salt, black pepper, and red pepper flakes if using.

Coat the Chickpeas:
- Add the chickpeas to the seasoning mixture and toss until they are well coated.

Spread on a Baking Sheet:
- Spread the seasoned chickpeas in a single layer on a baking sheet lined with parchment paper. Make sure they are not crowded to allow for even roasting.

Roast in the Oven:
- Roast the chickpeas in the preheated oven for about 25-30 minutes or until they are golden brown and crispy. Shake the pan or stir the chickpeas halfway through the cooking time for even crispiness.

Cool and Serve:

- Allow the roasted chickpeas to cool on the baking sheet for a few minutes before transferring them to a serving bowl. They will continue to crisp up as they cool.

Optional: Customize:
- Feel free to customize the seasoning to your liking. You can add a dash of cayenne pepper for extra heat or experiment with different herbs and spices.

Serve and Enjoy:
- Serve the Parmesan garlic roasted chickpeas as a snack or as a topping for salads. They're best enjoyed fresh, but you can store any leftovers in an airtight container for a day or two.

These Parmesan garlic roasted chickpeas are a flavorful and nutritious alternative to traditional snacks, offering a satisfying crunch with a burst of savory and cheesy goodness.

Peach and prosciutto flatbread

Ingredients:

- 1 pre-made flatbread or pizza crust
- 2 ripe peaches, thinly sliced
- 4-6 slices of prosciutto
- 1 cup fresh mozzarella, torn into small pieces
- 1/4 cup balsamic glaze
- 2 tablespoons olive oil
- 1/4 cup fresh basil leaves, torn
- Salt and pepper, to taste
- Optional: Arugula for garnish

Instructions:

Preheat the Oven:
- Preheat your oven according to the flatbread or pizza crust package instructions.

Prepare the Ingredients:
- Slice the ripe peaches thinly. Tear the fresh mozzarella into small pieces. Tear the prosciutto into bite-sized pieces. Tear the fresh basil leaves.

Assemble the Flatbread:
- Place the flatbread or pizza crust on a baking sheet. Brush the surface with olive oil.

Layer the Ingredients:
- Distribute the sliced peaches evenly over the flatbread. Scatter the torn mozzarella and prosciutto pieces over the peaches.

Bake in the Oven:
- Bake the flatbread in the preheated oven according to the crust's package instructions or until the edges are golden brown, and the cheese is melted and bubbly.

Drizzle with Balsamic Glaze:
- Once the flatbread is out of the oven, drizzle it with balsamic glaze. You can create a decorative pattern if you like.

Add Fresh Basil and Seasoning:
- Sprinkle torn fresh basil leaves over the flatbread. Add salt and pepper to taste.

Optional: Garnish with Arugula:

- For an extra layer of freshness and a peppery kick, you can garnish the flatbread with a handful of arugula just before serving.

Slice and Serve:
- Slice the peach and prosciutto flatbread into portions and serve immediately while it's warm.

This flatbread makes a fantastic appetizer or a light and flavorful meal. The combination of sweet peaches, salty prosciutto, and creamy mozzarella creates a harmonious blend of flavors. Enjoy this delicious dish as a refreshing addition to your menu!

Mini cheesecake bites

Ingredients:

For the Crust:

- 1 cup graham cracker crumbs
- 3 tablespoons unsalted butter, melted
- 1 tablespoon granulated sugar

For the Cheesecake Filling:

- 2 packages (16 ounces total) cream cheese, softened
- 2/3 cup granulated sugar
- 2 large eggs, room temperature
- 1 teaspoon vanilla extract
- 1/4 cup sour cream

For Topping (optional):

- Fruit compote, fruit preserves, or chocolate ganache

Instructions:

1. Preheat the Oven:

- Preheat your oven to 325°F (160°C). Line mini muffin tins with mini cupcake liners.

2. Prepare the Crust:

In a bowl, combine graham cracker crumbs, melted butter, and sugar. Mix until the crumbs are evenly coated.
Press about a tablespoon of the crust mixture into the bottom of each mini cupcake liner, creating a firm and even base.

3. Make the Cheesecake Filling:

In a mixing bowl, beat the cream cheese until smooth using an electric mixer.
Add the sugar and continue beating until well combined and smooth.
Add the eggs, one at a time, beating well after each addition. Scrape down the sides of the bowl as needed.
Mix in the vanilla extract and sour cream until the batter is smooth and creamy.

4. Fill the Mini Cupcake Liners:

    Spoon or pipe the cheesecake batter into each mini cupcake liner, filling almost to the top.
    Smooth the tops with the back of a spoon or a spatula.

5. Bake:

    - Bake in the preheated oven for about 12-15 minutes or until the edges are set, and the centers are slightly jiggly.

6. Cool and Chill:

    Allow the mini cheesecakes to cool in the muffin tins for a few minutes.
    Transfer them to a wire rack to cool completely, and then refrigerate for at least 2 hours or until fully chilled.

7. Add Toppings (Optional):

    - Once chilled, you can add your favorite toppings such as fruit compote, fruit preserves, or chocolate ganache.

8. Serve:

    - Carefully remove the mini cheesecake bites from the liners, and arrange them on a serving platter.

Enjoy these mini cheesecake bites as a delightful treat for parties, gatherings, or as a sweet indulgence anytime!

Sweet potato fries with garlic aioli

Ingredients:

For Sweet Potato Fries:

- 2 large sweet potatoes, peeled and cut into fries
- 2 tablespoons olive oil
- 1 teaspoon paprika
- 1 teaspoon garlic powder
- 1 teaspoon salt
- 1/2 teaspoon black pepper
- 1/2 teaspoon cayenne pepper (optional, for some heat)
- 1 tablespoon cornstarch (optional, for added crispiness)

For Garlic Aioli:

- 1/2 cup mayonnaise
- 2 cloves garlic, minced
- 1 tablespoon lemon juice
- 1 teaspoon Dijon mustard
- Salt and pepper, to taste

Instructions:

1. Preheat the Oven:

- Preheat your oven to 425°F (220°C). Line a baking sheet with parchment paper.

2. Prepare Sweet Potato Fries:

In a large bowl, toss the sweet potato fries with olive oil, paprika, garlic powder, salt, black pepper, and cayenne pepper until evenly coated.
If you want extra crispiness, you can toss the fries with cornstarch.
Spread the sweet potato fries in a single layer on the prepared baking sheet, ensuring they are not crowded for even cooking.

3. Bake:

- Bake in the preheated oven for 20-25 minutes or until the fries are golden brown and crispy, flipping them halfway through the cooking time.

4. Prepare Garlic Aioli:

    In a small bowl, combine mayonnaise, minced garlic, lemon juice, and Dijon mustard. Mix well.
    Season the garlic aioli with salt and pepper to taste. Adjust the ingredients to achieve your desired flavor.

5. Serve:

    - Once the sweet potato fries are done, transfer them to a serving plate. Serve the fries hot with the prepared garlic aioli on the side for dipping.

Enjoy these sweet potato fries with garlic aioli as a flavorful and satisfying snack or side dish. The combination of the slightly sweet fries and the creamy, garlicky aioli is sure to be a crowd-pleaser!

Pomegranate and goat cheese crostini

Ingredients:

- Baguette, sliced into 1/2-inch thick rounds
- Olive oil for brushing
- 1 cup goat cheese, softened
- 1 cup pomegranate seeds
- Honey for drizzling
- Fresh thyme leaves for garnish (optional)
- Salt and black pepper to taste

Instructions:

1. Preheat the Oven:

- Preheat your oven to 375°F (190°C).

2. Toast the Baguette Slices:

    Arrange the baguette slices on a baking sheet.
    Lightly brush each slice with olive oil.
    Toast the baguette slices in the preheated oven for about 8-10 minutes or until they are golden and crisp.

3. Prepare Goat Cheese Spread:

    In a bowl, mix the softened goat cheese until it's smooth and creamy.
    Season the goat cheese with a pinch of salt and black pepper, adjusting to taste.

4. Assemble the Crostini:

    Once the baguette slices are toasted, let them cool slightly.
    Spread a generous layer of goat cheese onto each toasted baguette slice.
    Sprinkle a few pomegranate seeds on top of the goat cheese.

5. Drizzle with Honey:

- Drizzle a small amount of honey over each crostini. The sweetness of the honey complements the tangy goat cheese and the burst of flavor from the pomegranate seeds.

6. Garnish and Serve:

- If desired, garnish the crostini with fresh thyme leaves for a touch of herbaceous flavor.
- Arrange the finished crostini on a serving platter and serve immediately.

These pomegranate and goat cheese crostini are a perfect combination of sweet, tangy, and creamy flavors, making them an elegant and crowd-pleasing appetizer for any occasion. Enjoy this colorful and delicious treat!

Honey mustard glazed chicken skewers

Ingredients:

For the Chicken Skewers:

- 1.5 lbs (about 700g) boneless, skinless chicken breasts, cut into bite-sized cubes
- Salt and black pepper, to taste
- 1 tablespoon olive oil

For the Honey Mustard Glaze:

- 1/4 cup Dijon mustard
- 3 tablespoons honey
- 2 tablespoons whole grain mustard
- 1 tablespoon soy sauce
- 1 teaspoon minced garlic
- 1 tablespoon olive oil
- Salt and black pepper, to taste

Other:

- Wooden skewers, soaked in water for at least 30 minutes

Instructions:

1. Prepare the Chicken Skewers:

    Season the chicken cubes with salt and black pepper. Drizzle with olive oil and toss until the chicken is evenly coated.
    Thread the chicken cubes onto the soaked wooden skewers, leaving a little space between each piece.
    Preheat your grill or grill pan to medium-high heat.
    Grill the chicken skewers for about 8-10 minutes, turning occasionally, or until the chicken is cooked through with a nice char on the outside.

2. Make the Honey Mustard Glaze:

    In a small saucepan over medium heat, combine Dijon mustard, honey, whole grain mustard, soy sauce, minced garlic, olive oil, salt, and black pepper.
    Whisk the mixture together and let it simmer for about 3-5 minutes, stirring frequently, until it thickens slightly.
    Remove the saucepan from the heat and set aside.

3. Glaze the Chicken Skewers:

   Brush the honey mustard glaze generously over the grilled chicken skewers during the last few minutes of cooking, allowing the glaze to caramelize.
   Continue turning the skewers and brushing with the glaze until the chicken is fully coated and has a beautiful golden-brown color.

4. Serve:

   - Once the chicken skewers are cooked and glazed, remove them from the grill.
   - Serve the honey mustard glazed chicken skewers warm, and you can optionally garnish with chopped fresh herbs, such as parsley or chives.

Enjoy these delicious honey mustard glazed chicken skewers as a tasty appetizer, party snack, or as part of a meal with your favorite sides!

Lemon poppy seed muffins

Ingredients:

Dry Ingredients:

- 2 cups all-purpose flour
- 3/4 cup granulated sugar
- 1 tablespoon poppy seeds
- 2 teaspoons baking powder
- 1/2 teaspoon baking soda
- 1/4 teaspoon salt

Wet Ingredients:

- 3/4 cup unsalted butter, melted and cooled
- 1 cup plain yogurt or sour cream
- 2 large eggs
- 1 teaspoon vanilla extract
- Zest of 2 lemons
- Juice of 1 lemon

Glaze (Optional):

- 1 cup powdered sugar
- 2-3 tablespoons lemon juice

Instructions:

1. Preheat the Oven:

- Preheat your oven to 375°F (190°C). Line a muffin tin with paper liners or grease the muffin cups.

2. Mix the Dry Ingredients:

In a large bowl, whisk together the flour, sugar, poppy seeds, baking powder, baking soda, and salt.

3. Mix the Wet Ingredients:

In another bowl, whisk together the melted butter, yogurt (or sour cream), eggs, vanilla extract, lemon zest, and lemon juice.
Pour the wet ingredients into the dry ingredients.

Gently fold the ingredients together until just combined. Be careful not to overmix; a few lumps are okay.

4. Fill the Muffin Cups:

    Divide the batter evenly among the prepared muffin cups, filling each about two-thirds full.

5. Bake:

    - Bake in the preheated oven for about 18-22 minutes or until a toothpick inserted into the center comes out clean or with a few moist crumbs.

6. Make the Glaze (Optional):

    While the muffins are baking, prepare the glaze by whisking together powdered sugar and lemon juice until smooth. Adjust the consistency by adding more sugar or juice if needed.

7. Glaze the Muffins:

    Once the muffins are done and still warm, drizzle the lemon glaze over the tops.

8. Cool and Serve:

    - Allow the lemon poppy seed muffins to cool in the muffin tin for a few minutes before transferring them to a wire rack to cool completely.

These lemon poppy seed muffins are perfect for breakfast, brunch, or a sweet snack. The combination of the bright citrus flavor and the crunch of poppy seeds makes them a delightful treat. Enjoy!

Caprese-stuffed avocados

Ingredients:

- 3 ripe avocados
- 1 cup cherry tomatoes, halved
- 1 cup fresh mozzarella balls (bocconcini), halved or quartered
- Fresh basil leaves, torn
- Balsamic glaze for drizzling
- Extra virgin olive oil for drizzling
- Salt and black pepper, to taste

Instructions:

1. Prepare the Avocados:

    Cut the avocados in half and remove the pits.
    If needed, scoop out a small portion of the avocado flesh to create a larger cavity for stuffing.

2. Prepare the Caprese Filling:

    In a bowl, combine the halved cherry tomatoes and mozzarella balls.
    Toss in torn fresh basil leaves.
    Drizzle the mixture with extra virgin olive oil and season with salt and black pepper. Gently toss to combine.

3. Stuff the Avocados:

    Spoon the Caprese filling into the hollowed-out portion of each avocado half.
    Press down slightly to ensure the filling is packed inside.

4. Garnish and Drizzle:

    Drizzle balsamic glaze over the stuffed avocados for a sweet and tangy finish.
    Garnish with additional torn basil leaves.

5. Serve:
   - Serve the Caprese-stuffed avocados immediately, either as an appetizer, side dish, or a light and refreshing snack.

This recipe combines the creamy texture of avocados with the classic flavors of Caprese, resulting in a delicious and visually appealing dish. It's perfect for summer gatherings or whenever you want a quick and elegant appetizer. Enjoy!

Salted caramel brownie bites

Ingredients:

For the Brownie Bites:

- 1/2 cup (1 stick) unsalted butter
- 1 cup granulated sugar
- 2 large eggs
- 1 teaspoon vanilla extract
- 1/3 cup unsweetened cocoa powder
- 1/2 cup all-purpose flour
- 1/4 teaspoon salt

For the Salted Caramel:

- 1 cup granulated sugar
- 6 tablespoons unsalted butter, cut into pieces
- 1/2 cup heavy cream
- 1 teaspoon sea salt (adjust to taste)

Instructions:

1. Preheat the Oven:

- Preheat your oven to 350°F (175°C). Grease or line a mini muffin tin.

2. Prepare the Brownie Batter:

In a medium-sized microwave-safe bowl, melt the butter.
Stir in the sugar, eggs, and vanilla extract until well combined.
Sift in the cocoa powder, flour, and salt. Mix until just combined. Be careful not to overmix.

3. Fill the Mini Muffin Tin:

Spoon the brownie batter into the mini muffin cups, filling each about two-thirds full.
Bake in the preheated oven for 10-12 minutes or until a toothpick inserted into the center comes out with a few moist crumbs.
Allow the brownie bites to cool in the tin for a few minutes before transferring them to a wire rack to cool completely.

4. Make the Salted Caramel:

In a medium saucepan over medium heat, melt the granulated sugar, stirring constantly with a heat-resistant spatula or wooden spoon. The sugar will clump first and then melt into a smooth amber-colored liquid.

Once the sugar is completely melted, add the butter, one piece at a time, stirring continuously until well combined.

Slowly pour in the heavy cream while stirring constantly. Be careful as the mixture may bubble up.

Continue to cook and stir for an additional 1-2 minutes until the caramel is smooth and slightly thickened.

Remove the saucepan from heat and stir in the sea salt. Allow the caramel to cool slightly.

5. Assemble the Brownie Bites:

Using your thumb or the back of a small spoon, create a small well in the center of each brownie bite.

Spoon or drizzle the salted caramel into the well, allowing it to fill the center.

6. Serve:

- Sprinkle a bit of additional sea salt on top if desired.
- Serve these salted caramel brownie bites on a platter and enjoy these delicious and indulgent treats!

These salted caramel brownie bites are perfect for parties, dessert tables, or whenever you're craving a sweet and salty treat. The combination of fudgy brownies and gooey caramel is sure to be a crowd-pleaser.

Roasted red pepper hummus

Ingredients:

- 1 can (15 ounces) chickpeas, drained and rinsed
- 1/2 cup roasted red peppers (from a jar or homemade)
- 1/4 cup tahini (sesame paste)
- 1/4 cup extra virgin olive oil
- 1 clove garlic, minced
- 1 tablespoon fresh lemon juice
- 1/2 teaspoon ground cumin
- Salt and black pepper, to taste
- Pinch of cayenne pepper (optional, for some heat)
- 2 tablespoons chopped fresh parsley (for garnish)

Instructions:

1. Roast Red Peppers (if not using jarred):

    Preheat your oven's broiler. Cut red peppers in half, remove seeds, and flatten them with your hand.
    Place the peppers, skin side up, on a baking sheet lined with parchment paper. Broil the peppers until the skins are blackened and blistered, about 10-15 minutes.
    Transfer the hot peppers to a bowl, cover with plastic wrap, and let them steam for about 10 minutes. Then, peel off the skin.

2. Prepare Hummus:

    In a food processor, combine chickpeas, roasted red peppers, tahini, olive oil, minced garlic, lemon juice, cumin, salt, black pepper, and cayenne pepper (if using).
    Process until the mixture is smooth and creamy. You may need to stop and scrape down the sides of the processor bowl a few times.
    Taste the hummus and adjust the seasoning if needed, adding more salt, pepper, or lemon juice according to your preference.

3. Serve:

    Transfer the roasted red pepper hummus to a serving bowl.

Drizzle with a bit of extra virgin olive oil and sprinkle chopped fresh parsley on top for garnish.
Serve the hummus with pita bread, fresh veggies, or your favorite crackers.

This roasted red pepper hummus is not only delicious but also adds a burst of color to your table. It's perfect for snacking, dipping, or as a spread on sandwiches. Enjoy!

Apple pecan brie bites

Ingredients:

- 1 sheet puff pastry, thawed
- 1 wheel of brie cheese (about 8 ounces)
- 1 medium apple (such as Granny Smith or Honeycrisp), thinly sliced
- 1/2 cup chopped pecans
- 2 tablespoons honey
- Fresh thyme leaves for garnish (optional)

Instructions:

1. Preheat the Oven:

- Preheat your oven to 375°F (190°C).

2. Prepare Puff Pastry:

    Roll out the puff pastry sheet on a lightly floured surface.
    Cut the puff pastry into small squares, approximately 2x2 inches.

3. Assemble Brie Bites:

    Place a small piece of brie (about 1-inch square) in the center of each puff pastry square.
    Top the brie with a slice of apple and a sprinkle of chopped pecans.
    Fold the corners of the puff pastry over the brie, creating a small, rustic-looking bundle.

4. Bake:

- Place the assembled brie bites on a parchment paper-lined baking sheet.
- Bake in the preheated oven for 12-15 minutes or until the puff pastry is golden brown and the brie is melted.

5. Drizzle with Honey:

    Remove the brie bites from the oven and immediately drizzle honey over each bite.
    Optionally, garnish with fresh thyme leaves for a touch of herbaceous flavor.

6. Serve:

- Allow the brie bites to cool slightly before serving.
- Arrange them on a serving platter and enjoy these delightful apple pecan brie bites as a tasty appetizer for parties or gatherings.

These bites are a perfect combination of sweet, creamy, and nutty flavors, making them a crowd-pleaser. They are great for entertaining or as a delicious treat for a cozy evening at home.

Mini key lime pies

Ingredients:

For the Graham Cracker Crust:

- 1 1/2 cups graham cracker crumbs
- 1/4 cup granulated sugar
- 1/2 cup unsalted butter, melted

For the Key Lime Filling:

- 4 large egg yolks
- 1 can (14 ounces) sweetened condensed milk
- 1/2 cup key lime juice (freshly squeezed if possible)
- Zest of 2 key limes

For Topping (Optional):

- Whipped cream
- Lime slices or zest for garnish

Instructions:

1. Preheat the Oven:

- Preheat your oven to 350°F (175°C).

2. Prepare the Graham Cracker Crust:

In a bowl, combine the graham cracker crumbs, sugar, and melted butter. Mix until the crumbs are evenly coated.
Press the mixture into the bottoms of a mini muffin tin to create a crust.

3. Bake the Crust:

- Bake the crust in the preheated oven for about 8-10 minutes or until it's set and lightly golden. Remove from the oven and let it cool while you prepare the filling.

4. Make the Key Lime Filling:

In a separate bowl, whisk together the egg yolks, sweetened condensed milk, key lime juice, and key lime zest until well combined.
Spoon or pour the key lime filling into the cooled graham cracker crusts.

5. Bake the Mini Key Lime Pies:
   - Bake the mini key lime pies in the preheated oven for approximately 10-12 minutes or until the edges are set but the center is still slightly jiggly.

6. Chill:
   - Allow the mini key lime pies to cool in the muffin tin, and then transfer them to the refrigerator to chill for at least 2 hours or until fully set.

7. Serve:
   - Once chilled, remove the mini key lime pies from the muffin tin and arrange them on a serving platter.
   - Optionally, top each mini pie with a dollop of whipped cream and garnish with lime slices or zest.

Enjoy these mini key lime pies as a delightful and tangy treat. They're perfect for parties, gatherings, or as a refreshing dessert on a warm day.

Bacon-wrapped jalapeño poppers

Ingredients:

- 12 fresh jalapeño peppers
- 8 ounces cream cheese, softened
- 1 cup shredded cheddar cheese
- 1 teaspoon garlic powder
- 1 teaspoon onion powder
- 1/2 teaspoon smoked paprika
- 12 slices of bacon, cut in half
- Toothpicks

Instructions:

1. Preheat the Oven:

- Preheat your oven to 375°F (190°C).

2. Prepare the Jalapeños:

Cut each jalapeño in half lengthwise, leaving the stems intact. Remove the seeds and membranes for a milder flavor or leave them for more heat.
In a bowl, combine cream cheese, shredded cheddar cheese, garlic powder, onion powder, and smoked paprika. Mix until well combined.
Fill each jalapeño half with the cheese mixture, smoothing the top.

3. Wrap with Bacon:

Take a half-slice of bacon and wrap it around each stuffed jalapeño, securing it with a toothpick.
Place the bacon-wrapped jalapeño poppers on a baking sheet lined with parchment paper.

4. Bake:

- Bake in the preheated oven for about 20-25 minutes or until the bacon is crispy and the jalapeños are tender.

5. Broil (Optional):

If you'd like the bacon to be even crispier, you can broil the poppers for an additional 1-2 minutes, keeping a close eye to prevent burning.

Remove the poppers from the oven.

6. Serve:

- Let the bacon-wrapped jalapeño poppers cool slightly before serving.
- Serve them on a platter, and enjoy these delicious and spicy appetizers!

These bacon-wrapped jalapeño poppers are a perfect party snack or game day treat. The combination of creamy cheese, spicy jalapeños, and crispy bacon is sure to be a crowd-pleaser. Remember to advise your guests about the potential heat of the jalapeños!

Nutella-filled crescent rolls

Ingredients:

- 1 can (8 oz) refrigerated crescent rolls
- Nutella (as needed)

Instructions:

Preheat your oven to the temperature specified on the crescent roll package.
Unroll the crescent dough on a clean surface and separate the triangles.
Take a teaspoon of Nutella and spread it onto each triangle, starting at the wide end and spreading towards the pointed end.
Roll up each crescent roll, starting from the wide end, and place them on a baking sheet lined with parchment paper, with the pointed end underneath to prevent them from unraveling.
Bake according to the instructions on the crescent roll package or until they are golden brown.
Once baked, allow the Nutella-filled crescent rolls to cool slightly before serving.
Optionally, you can sprinkle powdered sugar on top or drizzle with additional Nutella for extra sweetness.

Enjoy your delicious Nutella-filled crescent rolls! They make for a perfect breakfast, snack, or dessert.

Teriyaki chicken lettuce wraps

Ingredients:

For Teriyaki Chicken:

- 1 lb boneless, skinless chicken breasts, diced into small pieces
- 1/4 cup soy sauce
- 2 tablespoons honey
- 2 tablespoons rice vinegar
- 1 tablespoon mirin (sweet rice wine)
- 1 clove garlic, minced
- 1 teaspoon ginger, grated
- 1 tablespoon cornstarch (optional, for thickening)

For Lettuce Wraps:

- Large iceberg or butter lettuce leaves, washed and separated
- 1 cup cooked jasmine rice (optional)
- 1 cup diced vegetables (such as bell peppers, carrots, water chestnuts)
- Green onions, chopped (for garnish)
- Sesame seeds (for garnish)
- Soy sauce and sriracha (optional, for serving)

Instructions:

In a bowl, whisk together soy sauce, honey, rice vinegar, mirin, minced garlic, and grated ginger to make the teriyaki sauce.

Heat a bit of oil in a pan over medium heat. Add diced chicken and cook until browned and cooked through.

Pour the teriyaki sauce over the cooked chicken and stir well. If you prefer a thicker sauce, mix cornstarch with a little water to create a slurry, then add it to the pan and stir until the sauce thickens.

Once the chicken is coated in the teriyaki sauce and heated through, remove it from the heat.

Assemble the lettuce wraps by placing a spoonful of teriyaki chicken onto each lettuce leaf.

Top the chicken with cooked jasmine rice (if using), diced vegetables, green onions, and sesame seeds.

Serve the lettuce wraps with additional soy sauce and sriracha on the side for dipping, if desired.

Enjoy these delicious and flavorful teriyaki chicken lettuce wraps! They make for a refreshing and satisfying meal.

Pistachio and cranberry biscotti

Ingredients:

- 1 cup shelled pistachios, roughly chopped
- 1 cup dried cranberries
- 2¾ cups all-purpose flour
- 1½ teaspoons baking powder
- ½ teaspoon salt
- 4 large eggs
- 1 cup granulated sugar
- 1 teaspoon vanilla extract

Instructions:

Preheat your oven to 350°F (175°C). Line a baking sheet with parchment paper.
In a large bowl, whisk together the flour, baking powder, and salt.
In another bowl, beat the eggs, sugar, and vanilla extract until well combined.
Gradually add the dry ingredients to the wet ingredients, mixing until a dough forms.
Fold in the pistachios and dried cranberries until evenly distributed in the dough.
Divide the dough in half. On a floured surface, shape each half into a log about 12 inches long and 2 inches wide. Place the logs on the prepared baking sheet, leaving space between them.
Bake in the preheated oven for about 25-30 minutes, or until the logs are firm to the touch and lightly golden brown.
Remove the logs from the oven and let them cool for about 10 minutes. Reduce the oven temperature to 325°F (160°C).
Using a serrated knife, slice the logs diagonally into 1/2-inch-wide slices.
Arrange the slices on the baking sheet, cut sides down, and bake for an additional 10-15 minutes, or until the biscotti are golden and crisp.
Allow the biscotti to cool completely on a wire rack.

Once cooled, your pistachio and cranberry biscotti are ready to be enjoyed! These make for a delightful treat and are perfect for sharing or gifting.

Artichoke and parmesan dip

Ingredients:

- 1 can (14 oz) artichoke hearts, drained and chopped
- 1 cup mayonnaise
- 1 cup grated Parmesan cheese
- 1 cup shredded mozzarella cheese
- 1 clove garlic, minced
- 1 teaspoon lemon juice
- 1/2 teaspoon dried basil
- 1/4 teaspoon black pepper
- 1/4 teaspoon onion powder
- 1/4 teaspoon garlic powder
- Salt, to taste
- Optional: Chopped fresh parsley or chives for garnish

Instructions:

Preheat your oven to 350°F (175°C).
In a mixing bowl, combine the chopped artichoke hearts, mayonnaise, grated Parmesan cheese, shredded mozzarella cheese, minced garlic, lemon juice, dried basil, black pepper, onion powder, and garlic powder. Mix well until all ingredients are thoroughly combined.
Taste the mixture and adjust seasoning with salt if needed.
Transfer the mixture to a baking dish, spreading it evenly.
Bake in the preheated oven for about 25-30 minutes, or until the dip is hot and bubbly, and the top is golden brown.
If desired, garnish with chopped fresh parsley or chives before serving.
Serve the artichoke and Parmesan dip with tortilla chips, sliced baguette, or vegetable sticks for dipping.

This delicious dip is sure to be a hit at your next gathering. Enjoy the creamy texture and rich flavors of artichokes and Parmesan!

Chocolate chip cookie dough truffles

Ingredients:

For the Cookie Dough:

- 1/2 cup unsalted butter, softened
- 1/4 cup granulated sugar
- 1/2 cup packed light brown sugar
- 1 teaspoon vanilla extract
- 1 cup all-purpose flour
- 1/4 teaspoon salt
- 1/2 cup mini chocolate chips

For the Coating:

- 8 oz (about 1 1/2 cups) semi-sweet or milk chocolate, chopped
- 1 tablespoon vegetable oil

Instructions:

In a large mixing bowl, cream together the softened butter, granulated sugar, brown sugar, and vanilla extract until smooth and well combined.
Add the flour and salt to the mixture, and mix until a cookie dough forms.
Fold in the mini chocolate chips until evenly distributed throughout the dough.
Scoop small portions of the cookie dough (about 1 teaspoon each) and roll them into round truffle balls. Place the balls on a parchment-lined tray and freeze for about 15-20 minutes to firm them up.
While the cookie dough balls are in the freezer, melt the chocolate for coating. In a microwave-safe bowl or using a double boiler, melt the chopped chocolate with the vegetable oil, stirring until smooth.
Remove the cookie dough balls from the freezer. Using a fork or toothpick, dip each ball into the melted chocolate, making sure it is completely coated. Allow excess chocolate to drip off.
Place the coated truffles back on the parchment-lined tray and let them set at room temperature or in the refrigerator until the chocolate hardens.
Once the chocolate is fully set, transfer the truffles to an airtight container and store in the refrigerator until ready to serve.

Enjoy these delicious chocolate chip cookie dough truffles as a sweet treat or share them with friends and family. They're perfect for special occasions or when you're craving a bite-sized, cookie-dough-filled delight!

Greek salad cups

Ingredients:

For the Salad:

- Cherry tomatoes, halved
- Cucumber, diced
- Kalamata olives, pitted and sliced
- Feta cheese, crumbled
- Red onion, finely chopped
- Fresh oregano, chopped (or dried oregano)
- Salt and pepper, to taste
- Olive oil, for drizzling
- Lemon juice, for drizzling

For the Cups:

- Mini phyllo pastry cups (available in the frozen section of most grocery stores)

Instructions:

In a bowl, combine the cherry tomatoes, diced cucumber, sliced Kalamata olives, crumbled feta cheese, finely chopped red onion, and chopped fresh oregano. Drizzle olive oil and lemon juice over the salad mixture. Season with salt and pepper to taste. Toss the salad gently until all the ingredients are well combined.
Preheat the mini phyllo pastry cups according to the package instructions (usually for a few minutes in the oven).
Once the pastry cups are ready, fill each cup with a spoonful of the Greek salad mixture.
Arrange the filled cups on a serving platter.
Optionally, garnish with additional crumbled feta and a sprinkle of fresh oregano on top.
Serve the Greek salad cups immediately, or refrigerate for a short time before serving if you prefer them chilled.

These Greek salad cups are not only delicious but also visually appealing. They make a great appetizer for parties or a light and flavorful snack. Enjoy the combination of crisp phyllo cups with the vibrant and classic Greek salad ingredients!

Raspberry cheesecake bars

Ingredients:

For the Crust:

- 1 1/2 cups graham cracker crumbs
- 1/3 cup unsalted butter, melted
- 1/4 cup granulated sugar

For the Cheesecake Filling:

- 16 oz (2 blocks) cream cheese, softened
- 2/3 cup granulated sugar
- 2 large eggs
- 1 teaspoon vanilla extract

For the Raspberry Swirl:

- 1 cup fresh raspberries
- 2 tablespoons granulated sugar
- 1 teaspoon cornstarch

Instructions:

Preheat your oven to 325°F (163°C). Line a 9x9-inch baking pan with parchment paper, leaving some overhang on the sides for easy removal.
In a medium bowl, combine the graham cracker crumbs, melted butter, and sugar for the crust. Press the mixture into the bottom of the prepared pan to create an even layer.
In a large bowl, beat the softened cream cheese until smooth using an electric mixer.
Add the granulated sugar, eggs, and vanilla extract to the cream cheese. Continue to beat until well combined and smooth.
Pour the cream cheese mixture over the crust in the baking pan, spreading it evenly.
In a blender or food processor, puree the raspberries until smooth. Strain the puree through a fine-mesh sieve into a bowl to remove the seeds.

In a small saucepan, combine the raspberry puree, sugar, and cornstarch. Cook over medium heat, stirring constantly, until the mixture thickens. Remove from heat and let it cool slightly.

Spoon dollops of the raspberry mixture onto the cream cheese layer. Use a knife or skewer to swirl the raspberry mixture into the cream cheese, creating a marbled pattern.

Bake in the preheated oven for about 35-40 minutes or until the edges are set and the center is slightly jiggly.

Allow the raspberry cheesecake bars to cool completely in the pan before refrigerating for at least 3-4 hours or overnight.

Once chilled, use the parchment paper overhangs to lift the bars out of the pan. Place them on a cutting board and slice into squares.

Serve chilled and enjoy your delicious raspberry cheesecake bars!

These bars are a delightful combination of creamy cheesecake and fruity raspberry swirls, making them a perfect treat for any occasion.

Spicy honey glazed shrimp

Ingredients:

- 1 pound large shrimp, peeled and deveined
- 2 tablespoons honey
- 2 tablespoons soy sauce
- 1 tablespoon Sriracha or your favorite hot sauce (adjust to taste)
- 2 cloves garlic, minced
- 1 teaspoon ginger, grated
- 1 tablespoon vegetable oil
- Salt and black pepper, to taste
- Green onions, chopped (for garnish)
- Sesame seeds (for garnish)

Instructions:

In a small bowl, whisk together honey, soy sauce, Sriracha, minced garlic, and grated ginger to create the glaze. Set aside.
Pat the shrimp dry with paper towels and season them with salt and black pepper.
Heat vegetable oil in a large skillet or wok over medium-high heat.
Add the shrimp to the skillet and cook for 1-2 minutes on each side, or until they start to turn pink and opaque.
Pour the honey glaze over the shrimp and toss to coat them evenly. Continue cooking for an additional 2-3 minutes, or until the shrimp are fully cooked and coated in the glaze.
Remove the skillet from heat.
Garnish the spicy honey glazed shrimp with chopped green onions and sesame seeds.
Serve the shrimp over rice, noodles, or as an appetizer with toothpicks for easy handling.

This dish offers a perfect balance of sweet and spicy flavors, making it a crowd-pleaser. Enjoy your spicy honey glazed shrimp as a flavorful main course or appetizer!

Caramel apple hand pies

Ingredients:

For the Filling:

- 2 cups peeled, cored, and diced apples (such as Granny Smith)
- 1/4 cup granulated sugar
- 1/4 cup brown sugar
- 1 tablespoon all-purpose flour
- 1 teaspoon ground cinnamon
- 1/4 teaspoon ground nutmeg
- 1/4 cup caramel sauce (plus extra for drizzling)

For the Crust:

- 2 store-bought pie crusts (or homemade if preferred)

For Assembly:

- 1 egg (for egg wash)
- 1 tablespoon water
- Granulated sugar (for sprinkling)

Instructions:

Preheat your oven to 375°F (190°C). Line a baking sheet with parchment paper. In a medium bowl, combine the diced apples, granulated sugar, brown sugar, flour, cinnamon, nutmeg, and caramel sauce. Mix well until the apples are evenly coated. Set aside.

Roll out the pie crusts on a lightly floured surface. Using a round cookie cutter or a glass, cut out circles from the crusts.

Place a spoonful of the apple filling in the center of each pie crust circle, leaving a small border around the edges.

Fold the circles in half over the filling, creating a semi-circle shape. Press the edges together to seal. You can use a fork to crimp the edges for a decorative touch.

In a small bowl, whisk together the egg and water to create an egg wash.

Place the assembled hand pies on the prepared baking sheet. Brush each pie with the egg wash and sprinkle with granulated sugar.

Using a small knife, make a couple of small slits on the top of each hand pie to allow steam to escape.
Bake in the preheated oven for 18-20 minutes or until the pies are golden brown.
Allow the hand pies to cool slightly before drizzling with extra caramel sauce.

These caramel apple hand pies are perfect for individual servings and make a delicious autumn treat. Enjoy them warm with a scoop of vanilla ice cream for an extra indulgence!

Mini chicken pot pies

Ingredients:

For the Filling:

- 1 cup cooked chicken, shredded or diced
- 1 cup frozen mixed vegetables (peas, carrots, corn, green beans), thawed
- 1/3 cup butter
- 1/3 cup all-purpose flour
- 1/2 teaspoon salt
- 1/4 teaspoon black pepper
- 1/4 teaspoon onion powder
- 1/4 teaspoon garlic powder
- 1/4 teaspoon dried thyme
- 1 3/4 cups chicken broth
- 2/3 cup milk

For the Crust:

- 2 sheets of refrigerated pie crust or homemade pie dough

Instructions:

Preheat your oven to 425°F (220°C). Grease a muffin tin or use cupcake liners.
In a medium saucepan, melt the butter over medium heat. Add the flour, salt, pepper, onion powder, garlic powder, and dried thyme. Stir constantly until the mixture is well combined and begins to bubble.
Gradually whisk in the chicken broth and milk, making sure to eliminate any lumps. Continue stirring until the mixture thickens. Remove the saucepan from the heat.
Add the cooked chicken and mixed vegetables to the sauce, stirring until everything is evenly coated.
Roll out the pie crust on a floured surface. Using a round cutter or a glass, cut out circles that will fit into the muffin tin cups.
Press the pie crust circles into the bottom and up the sides of each muffin cup, forming mini pie crusts.
Spoon the chicken and vegetable filling into each pie crust.

Roll out the remaining pie crust and cut smaller circles or strips to create a lattice pattern for the top of each mini pie.
Place the pies on a baking sheet and bake in the preheated oven for 15-20 minutes or until the crust is golden brown.
Allow the mini chicken pot pies to cool for a few minutes before serving.

These mini chicken pot pies are not only delicious but also perfect for portion control. They make a great appetizer for parties or a convenient lunch or dinner option. Enjoy!

Cheddar and chive potato skins

Ingredients:

- 4 large russet potatoes, scrubbed and dried
- 2 tablespoons olive oil
- Salt and black pepper, to taste
- 1 1/2 cups shredded cheddar cheese
- 1/4 cup chopped fresh chives
- Sour cream (for serving)

Instructions:

Preheat your oven to 400°F (200°C).
Pierce the potatoes with a fork in a few places. Place them directly on the oven rack and bake for about 45-60 minutes, or until the potatoes are fork-tender.
Allow the potatoes to cool slightly so they can be handled.
Cut the potatoes in half lengthwise. Scoop out the insides, leaving about 1/4 inch of potato attached to the skin. Save the scooped-out potato for another use (such as mashed potatoes).
Brush the inside and outside of each potato skin with olive oil. Season with salt and black pepper.
Place the potato skins on a baking sheet, skin side down. Bake in the preheated oven for about 10-15 minutes or until they become crispy.
Remove the potato skins from the oven and sprinkle each with shredded cheddar cheese.
Return the potato skins to the oven and bake for an additional 5-7 minutes, or until the cheese is melted and bubbly.
Remove the potato skins from the oven and sprinkle them with chopped fresh chives.
Serve the cheddar and chive potato skins with a side of sour cream for dipping.

These cheddar and chive potato skins are a crowd-pleasing appetizer, perfect for parties or game day gatherings. Enjoy the crispy texture and savory flavors!

Blueberry goat cheese crostini

Ingredients:

- Baguette or French bread, sliced into 1/2-inch thick rounds
- Olive oil, for brushing
- 8 oz goat cheese, softened
- 1 cup fresh blueberries
- Honey, for drizzling
- Fresh mint leaves, for garnish (optional)
- Balsamic glaze, for drizzling (optional)

Instructions:

Preheat your oven to 375°F (190°C).
Place the baguette slices on a baking sheet. Brush one side of each slice with olive oil.
Bake the bread slices in the preheated oven for about 8-10 minutes, or until they are golden and crispy. Remove from the oven and let them cool.
In a small bowl, mix the softened goat cheese until it becomes smooth and spreadable.
Once the crostini slices are cooled, spread a generous layer of goat cheese on the toasted side of each slice.
Top each crostini with a few fresh blueberries. Press them slightly into the goat cheese to adhere.
Drizzle honey over the blueberries, and if desired, add a few fresh mint leaves for garnish.
Optionally, you can also drizzle a balsamic glaze over the crostini for a touch of acidity and complexity.
Arrange the blueberry goat cheese crostini on a serving platter and serve immediately.

These blueberry goat cheese crostini are not only visually appealing but also a delightful combination of flavors and textures. They make an excellent appetizer for brunches, parties, or any special occasion. Enjoy!

Cinnamon sugar apple chips

Ingredients:

- 4-5 medium-sized apples (choose a sweet variety like Honeycrisp or Gala)
- 2 tablespoons granulated sugar
- 1-2 teaspoons ground cinnamon
- Cooking spray or parchment paper

Instructions:

Preheat your oven to 225°F (110°C). Line two baking sheets with parchment paper or lightly grease them with cooking spray.
Wash and thinly slice the apples, removing the cores and seeds. Using a mandoline or a sharp knife, aim for slices about 1/8 inch thick. Thinner slices will yield crispier chips.
In a bowl, combine the granulated sugar and ground cinnamon. Mix well.
Arrange the apple slices in a single layer on the prepared baking sheets. Ensure that the slices do not overlap.
Sprinkle the cinnamon sugar mixture evenly over the apple slices.
Bake in the preheated oven for 1.5 to 2 hours, or until the apple chips are crisp and lightly golden brown. Flip the slices halfway through the baking time to ensure even crisping.
Keep a close eye on them towards the end of the baking time, as the thickness of the slices and your oven's temperature may vary.
Once the apple chips are done, remove them from the oven and let them cool on the baking sheets. They will continue to crisp up as they cool.
Store the cinnamon sugar apple chips in an airtight container. They are best enjoyed within a day or two to maintain their crispiness.

These homemade cinnamon sugar apple chips are a healthy and flavorful alternative to store-bought snacks. They are perfect for satisfying your sweet tooth while providing the natural goodness of apples. Enjoy!

BBQ pulled pork sliders

Ingredients:

For the Pulled Pork:

- 3 to 4 pounds pork shoulder or pork butt
- Salt and black pepper, to taste
- 1 tablespoon olive oil
- 1 large onion, finely chopped
- 3 cloves garlic, minced
- 1 cup barbecue sauce (plus extra for serving)
- 1 cup chicken or vegetable broth
- 1 tablespoon Dijon mustard
- 1 tablespoon Worcestershire sauce
- 1 teaspoon smoked paprika
- 1/2 teaspoon cayenne pepper (optional, for added heat)

For the Sliders:

- Slider buns or small dinner rolls
- Coleslaw (optional, for topping)

Instructions:

Preheat your oven to 300°F (150°C).
Season the pork shoulder or pork butt with salt and black pepper.
In a large oven-safe pot or Dutch oven, heat the olive oil over medium-high heat. Brown the pork on all sides until it forms a nice crust. Remove the pork from the pot and set it aside.
In the same pot, add chopped onions and sauté until softened, about 3-4 minutes. Add minced garlic and sauté for an additional 1 minute.
Place the browned pork back into the pot. Add barbecue sauce, chicken or vegetable broth, Dijon mustard, Worcestershire sauce, smoked paprika, and cayenne pepper (if using). Stir to combine.
Cover the pot with a lid and transfer it to the preheated oven. Bake for 3 to 4 hours or until the pork is tender and easily shreds with a fork.
Remove the pork from the pot and shred it using two forks. Mix the shredded pork with the remaining cooking juices and barbecue sauce.

Toast the slider buns or dinner rolls in the oven or on a grill for a couple of minutes.

Assemble the sliders by placing a generous amount of pulled pork on the bottom half of each bun. Top with coleslaw if desired, and cover with the other half of the bun.

Serve the BBQ pulled pork sliders with extra barbecue sauce on the side.

These sliders are sure to be a hit with their tender and flavorful pulled pork. They're great for entertaining, and the coleslaw adds a refreshing crunch. Enjoy!

Nutella banana spring rolls

Ingredients:

- 8 spring roll wrappers (available in the Asian section of most grocery stores)
- 2 large ripe bananas, sliced
- Nutella (as needed)
- Oil, for frying
- Powdered sugar, for dusting (optional)
- Vanilla ice cream, for serving (optional)

Instructions:

Lay out one spring roll wrapper on a clean surface, with one corner facing you (diamond shape).
Place a few banana slices in the center of the wrapper.
Spoon a generous amount of Nutella over the banana slices.
Fold the bottom corner of the wrapper over the filling, then fold in the sides and roll it up tightly into a neat spring roll.
Seal the edge with a little water to make sure the spring roll stays closed.
Repeat the process with the remaining wrappers, bananas, and Nutella.
Heat oil in a pan or deep fryer to 350°F (180°C).
Carefully place the spring rolls in the hot oil and fry until they are golden brown and crispy, turning occasionally for even cooking. This usually takes about 2-3 minutes.
Remove the spring rolls from the oil and place them on a paper towel-lined plate to absorb any excess oil.
Optional: Dust the Nutella banana spring rolls with powdered sugar for an extra touch of sweetness.
Serve the spring rolls warm, either on their own or with a scoop of vanilla ice cream for a delightful contrast of hot and cold.

Enjoy these Nutella banana spring rolls as a delicious treat for dessert or a sweet snack.

The combination of Nutella and banana inside a crispy shell is sure to satisfy your sweet cravings!

Bacon-wrapped figs with goat cheese

Ingredients:

- Fresh figs, halved
- Goat cheese (enough to fill each fig half)
- Bacon slices (one slice per fig half)
- Balsamic glaze, for drizzling (optional)
- Toothpicks, for securing the bacon

Instructions:

Preheat your oven to 375°F (190°C).
Cut fresh figs in half and scoop out a small portion of the flesh from each half to make room for the goat cheese.
Take a small amount of goat cheese and fill each fig half with it.
Wrap each goat cheese-filled fig half with a slice of bacon. Secure the bacon with toothpicks, placing them through the bacon and into the fig to hold everything together.
Place the bacon-wrapped figs on a baking sheet lined with parchment paper or a baking rack.
Bake in the preheated oven for about 15-20 minutes, or until the bacon is crispy.
If desired, you can finish the bacon-wrapped figs under the broiler for an additional 1-2 minutes to crisp up the bacon even more.
Remove the toothpicks before serving.
Optional: Drizzle the bacon-wrapped figs with balsamic glaze for a sweet and tangy finish.

Serve these bacon-wrapped figs with goat cheese as a delicious appetizer at your next gathering. The combination of flavors is sure to impress your guests!

Lemon rosemary roasted nuts

Ingredients:

- 2 cups mixed nuts (such as almonds, walnuts, pecans, and cashews)
- 1 tablespoon fresh rosemary, finely chopped
- Zest of one lemon
- 2 tablespoons olive oil
- 1 tablespoon honey
- 1/2 teaspoon cayenne pepper (adjust to taste)
- Salt, to taste

Instructions:

Preheat your oven to 325°F (163°C). Line a baking sheet with parchment paper.
In a large bowl, combine the mixed nuts, chopped rosemary, lemon zest, olive oil, honey, cayenne pepper, and a pinch of salt. Mix well to ensure the nuts are evenly coated.
Spread the nut mixture evenly on the prepared baking sheet.
Roast in the preheated oven for about 15-20 minutes, stirring the nuts halfway through the cooking time to ensure even roasting.
Keep a close eye on the nuts, as they can quickly go from perfectly roasted to burnt.
Once the nuts are golden brown and fragrant, remove them from the oven and let them cool on the baking sheet.
Sprinkle with a bit more salt if needed while the nuts are still warm.
Allow the lemon rosemary roasted nuts to cool completely before transferring them to an airtight container for storage.

These nuts make for a wonderful snack on their own, or you can use them to top salads or serve as part of a charcuterie board. The combination of lemon and rosemary adds a refreshing and herby twist to the roasted nuts. Enjoy!

Pesto and sun-dried tomato pinwheels

Ingredients:

- 1 sheet of puff pastry, thawed if frozen
- 1/4 cup prepared pesto sauce
- 1/4 cup sun-dried tomatoes, chopped
- 1/2 cup shredded mozzarella cheese
- 1 egg, beaten (for egg wash)
- Fresh basil leaves, for garnish (optional)

Instructions:

Preheat your oven to the temperature specified on the puff pastry package (usually around 400°F or 200°C). Line a baking sheet with parchment paper.
Roll out the puff pastry sheet on a lightly floured surface to flatten it slightly.
Spread a thin layer of pesto sauce evenly over the entire surface of the puff pastry.
Sprinkle the chopped sun-dried tomatoes and shredded mozzarella cheese evenly over the pesto.
Starting from one edge, tightly roll the puff pastry into a log or cylinder.
Place the rolled puff pastry in the refrigerator for about 10-15 minutes to firm up, making it easier to slice.
Once chilled, remove the puff pastry log from the refrigerator and slice it into 1/2-inch thick pinwheels.
Place the pinwheels on the prepared baking sheet, leaving some space between each.
Brush the tops of the pinwheels with beaten egg, which will give them a golden color when baked.
Bake in the preheated oven for 12-15 minutes or until the pinwheels are puffed and golden brown.
Optional: Garnish with fresh basil leaves before serving.

These pesto and sun-dried tomato pinwheels are a delightful combination of flavors and textures. They are great for parties, gatherings, or as a tasty snack. Enjoy!

Cranberry orange shortbread cookies

Ingredients:

- 1 cup unsalted butter, softened
- 1/2 cup powdered sugar
- 1 teaspoon vanilla extract
- 2 cups all-purpose flour
- 1/2 cup dried cranberries, chopped
- Zest of 1 orange
- 1/4 teaspoon salt

For the Glaze (optional):

- 1 cup powdered sugar
- 2-3 tablespoons fresh orange juice

Instructions:

In a large bowl, cream together the softened butter and powdered sugar until light and fluffy.
Add the vanilla extract, orange zest, and salt. Mix until well combined.
Gradually add the flour to the butter mixture, mixing until a soft dough forms.
Fold in the chopped dried cranberries, ensuring they are evenly distributed throughout the dough.
Divide the dough in half and shape each half into a log about 1.5 inches in diameter. Wrap the logs in plastic wrap and refrigerate for at least 2 hours, or until firm.
Preheat your oven to 350°F (175°C). Line baking sheets with parchment paper.
Slice the chilled logs into 1/4-inch thick rounds and place them on the prepared baking sheets, leaving space between each cookie.
Bake in the preheated oven for 12-15 minutes, or until the edges of the cookies are golden brown.
Allow the cookies to cool on the baking sheets for a few minutes before transferring them to a wire rack to cool completely.

For the Glaze (optional):

In a small bowl, whisk together the powdered sugar and fresh orange juice until smooth.
Drizzle the glaze over the cooled cookies.
Allow the glaze to set before serving.

These cranberry orange shortbread cookies are perfect for holiday celebrations or any time you're craving a delightful combination of flavors. Enjoy the buttery, citrusy, and tart goodness!

Teriyaki pineapple chicken skewers

Ingredients:

For the Teriyaki Marinade:

- 1/2 cup soy sauce
- 1/4 cup water
- 3 tablespoons brown sugar
- 2 tablespoons honey
- 2 cloves garlic, minced
- 1 tablespoon ginger, grated
- 1 tablespoon sesame oil
- 1 tablespoon rice vinegar
- 1 tablespoon cornstarch (optional, for thickening)

For the Skewers:

- 1.5 lbs boneless, skinless chicken breasts, cut into bite-sized cubes
- 1 cup pineapple chunks (fresh or canned)
- Bell peppers, red onion, or other vegetables of your choice, cut into chunks
- Wooden or metal skewers

Instructions:

If using wooden skewers, soak them in water for about 30 minutes to prevent them from burning during grilling.

In a bowl, whisk together all the teriyaki marinade ingredients until well combined. If you prefer a thicker marinade, you can add cornstarch to the mixture and whisk until smooth.

Place the chicken cubes in a large resealable plastic bag or a shallow dish. Pour half of the teriyaki marinade over the chicken, reserving the other half for basting and serving later.

Marinate the chicken in the refrigerator for at least 30 minutes, or ideally, a few hours to let the flavors develop.

Preheat your grill or grill pan to medium-high heat.

Thread the marinated chicken, pineapple chunks, and vegetables onto the skewers, alternating between them.

Grill the skewers for about 8-10 minutes, turning occasionally, or until the chicken is cooked through and has a nice char on the edges.

During the last few minutes of grilling, brush the skewers with the reserved teriyaki marinade for extra flavor.

Once the chicken is cocked through and the vegetables are tender, remove the skewers from the grill.

Serve the teriyaki pineapple chicken skewers over rice or noodles, and drizzle with any remaining teriyaki sauce. Garnish with sesame seeds and chopped green onions if desired.

These teriyaki pineapple chicken skewers are perfect for a barbecue or a quick and flavorful weeknight dinner. Enjoy the combination of sweet pineapple and savory teriyaki-marinated chicken!